NICOTEXT

Truth or Dare

Copyright © NICOTEXT 2010 All rights reserved.
NICOTEXT part of Cladd media ltd.
www.nicotext.com
info@nicotext.com

Printed in the USA
ISBN: 978-91-86283-11-7

DO NOT DRINK AND DRIVE & DO NOT DRINK ALCOHOL
IF YOU ARE UNDER DRINKING AGE!

...AND KIDS, REMEMBER, ALWAYS WEAR A CONDOM!

Rules:

Truth or Dare is a piece of cake. First, simply pop the question: "Truth or dare?"

Then flip through the pages until you feel like stopping, but no reading the text before you do. Alternatively, simply say a number between 8 and 207, where even numbers are Dare's and odd numbers Truth's.

There shall be no lying, cheating or otherwise avoiding embarrassing questions and dares. Or else a very bad man will find you when you go to sleep tonight.

Dare

Lick something the other players choose.

If you were invisible, what would the first thing you would do?

9

Dare

Let the person you know the least send a text to someone in your phonebook.

10

If you could find out something about the future, what would it be?

11

Dare

Give everyone some advice on how to behave.

Truth

If you were convicted for a crime of passion, what would your crime be?

15

Dare

Try to pick up the person to the right of you.

16

Which family member would you want
to date a person in this room?

17

Dare

Kiss the person you like the most.

Truth

Have you ever lied about how you voted?

19

Dare

Let the person two steps to the right slap you.

20

When was the last time you changed your sheets?

21

Dare

Let the player sitting furthest away mix you a drink.

22

If you could ask someone in this room one question, and they had to answer honestly, who and what would you ask?

Dare

Give a random player a French kiss.

Are there naked pictures of you on the Internet?

Dare

Give all the players a hickey.

28

If you had to kill one person instantly, in a very painful, brutal way with a chainsaw, who would it be?

29

Dare

Tickle another player until he or she laughs out loud.

30

What's the biggest age difference between you and someone you've made out with?

31

Dare

Whisper something dirty to the player to the right. He or she passes it over to the next one until it comes back to you. Say it out loud.

32

Truth

Let the person sitting directly to the left of you ask you a question. You have to answer it honestly.

Dare

Guess what size jeans all the other players have.

What's the strangest sex position you have ever tried?

Dare

Burp the alphabet.

Confess something you have stolen recently.

41

Dare

Give every player a kiss on the mouth.

42

What's the stupidest thing you've done while drunk?

Dare

Get out on the pretend catwalk and show your stuff.

What is the most public place you have had sex?

45

Dare

Dance a slow dance with the person three steps to the right.

Truth

What's the most unfaithful act you've done?

Dare

Suck random finger on the player three steps to your right.

If you were a meal, how would you describe yourself?

57

Dare

Drink something while upside down.

Which of your physical attributes do you get the most compliments for?

61

Dare

Give the person to your right a bear hug (everlasting hug) for 3 minutes.

What physical insecurities do you have?

Dare

Open a door or a window and scream:
"I'm a monster and you're my prey!"

64

Truth

Have you ever lied about your age?

65

Dare

Do the robot dance.

Who of the players is most likely to have a baby first?

67

Dare

Let the person two steps to the right write something on your bum.

What's the silliest thing you have done to impress someone?

71

Dare

Make a player an offer he or she can't refuse.

Have you ever made a move on someone you knew your friend was interested in?

Dare

Try to pick up the other players with your absolute best pick-up lines.

Have you ever eaten something from the garbage?

Dare

Act like a judge for 5 minutes onward.

Have you ever examined your poop after pooping?

Dare

Comment on all actions in the room like a sports commentator for the next 10 minutes.

84

What prejudice do you have about the other sex that you are pretty much convinced is true?

Dare

Make everyone change places with each other.

Have you ever sniffed your underwear to see if they're clean?

Dare

Act like a real gentleman toward everybody for the rest of the game.

06

Have you ever crossed the line in some way with a friend's ex or partner?

Dare

Call your mom and tell her you love her.

If someone asks you for your opinion on how they look, do you answer honestly if you think they look awful?

Dare

Juggle with at least three things in this room.

What's the best present you ever got?
The worst?

Dare

Give someone an Eskimo kiss.

When was the last time you told someone you loved them? Who had the honor?

103

Dare

Talk backwards for ten minutes,
like the log lady from Twin Peaks.

What do you brag about?

Dare

Sing your favorite song and break loose a little dance.

If push came to shove, who would you most likely make out with in this room?

Dare

Pick the nose of the person sitting three steps to the left of you.

110

Have you ever had a rebound relationship/sex?

Dare

Call a person that the other players choose and tell him/her you have a crush on them.

112

Name one person in the room you are jealous of and give reason why.

113

Dare

Go ask the neighbor for a cup of sugar.

114

Who are you in love with at the moment?
Who do you have the hots for?

Dare

Challenge a person in a staring contest (stare at each other, the person who starts laughing first loses).

What's the meanest thing you've done
to a lover?

Dare

Repeat everything everyone says until it's your turn again.

Which two would be the oddest love couple
in the room? Why?

Dare

Pretend you are an aerobics instructor and give the other players a one minute work out.

124

Have you ever worn your underwear for more than one day? Have you ever turned your underwear inside out to make them last longer?

125

Dare

Do the Macarena!

What are you insecure about right now?

Dare

Close your eyes and let the other players find something in the kitchen you must have a taste of.

Do you believe in god? Will you go to heaven or hell?

Dare

Propose to the person you would most likely marry in the room.

132

Are you a good tipper?

Dare

Talk one of the players into having a child with you.

134

On a scale from 1 to 10, how good-looking do you think you are?

Dare

Let the person on your right mess up your hair.

Which drug do you think should be legal in this country?

Dare

Challenge the person two steps to the left at something

This room is on fire and you can save everyone except one person. Who would you leave behind?

Dare

Give the person to your left a backrub until it's your turn again.

Truth

How many people have you made out with?

143

Dare

Try to fit all the players into the smallest space available.

Have you ever stolen something from your workplace? What?

Dare

Try to sell your dirty socks for the highest price you can get. You must get something for them.

What's the meanest way you have ever treated an animal?

151

Dare

Let the other players write something on your Facebook wall. If you don't have Facebook they may send an e-mail from your address to a person of their choice.

152

Tell something about yourself that none of the other players knows about you. You have to keep doing it until everyone agrees that they didn't know about it

153

Dare

Drink 3 glasses of water in 5 minutes.

154

Have you ever lied when playing truth or dare?

Dare

Lick a random person's ear.

What would you do if you found yourself without toilet paper after taking a dump?

Dare

Smell everyone's breath and tell who's got worst.

If you had to switch apartments with one of the players forever, whom would you switch with?

Dare

Call someone and claim you're being kidnapped. Really convince them.

What do many people call you, and what do you think about your nickname?

Dare

Imitate someone from the Simpson family.

What competition are you most likely to win over the other players?

Dare

Make a toast for a pretend wedding couple.

172

Which player would you never choose as a roommate?

Dare

Take out all your money from your wallet and count it in front of the other players. If you don't have any let the players inspect your wallet.

174

Have you had any STDs?

Dare

Whistle a song until the other players guess what song it is.

When was the last time you got into a fight?
What was it about?

Dare

Show everyone how flexible you are.

Have you ever cheated in something really serious?

183

Dare

Misunderstand everything that the others are telling you.

What sexual act do you regret the most?

Dare

Massage the person across from you in a sensual way.

Your house is on fire and you only have time to save one thing? What would it be?

Dare

Do 10 push ups. Slowly.

Give every player a sincere compliment

189

Dare

Make someone in the room blush.

Have you ever experienced something supernatural?
Do tell.

191

Dare

Touch another player's tongue with your tongue.

Have you ever used a baby voice while talking to a lover/girlfriend/boyfriend?

193

Dare

Put your earlobe in someone's mouth.

Have you ever stolen anything that cost more than you could afford?

Dare

Moon your neighbors.

Have you ever made out or had sex with a teacher, boss or other superior?

197

Dare

Describe your latest sexual experience in detail.

Have you ever broken any laws?
Name them.

Dare

Pretend like you don't know the participant opposite you and try to pick him/her up.

200

When are you invincible?

Dare

Rub your bum against someone's crotch.

202

Tell every player what your first impression of him or her was.

203

Dare

Drink something from the belly button of a random player.

204

Who are you avoiding? For what reason?

Dare

Rub your body against all the other players.

206

If you could be a movie character for a week, who would it be?